KT-383-859

Text copyright © 2006 by Melanie Mitchell

All rights reserved. International copyright secured. No part of this book may be reproduced, stored in a retrieval system or transmitted in any form or by any means – electronic, mechanical, photocopying, recording or otherwise – without the prior written permission of Lerner Publishing Group, Inc., except for the inclusion of brief quotations in an acknowledged review.

This book was first published in the United States of America in 2006.

First published in the United Kingdom in 2008 by
Lerner Books,
Dalton House,
60 Windsor Avenue,
London SW19 2RR

Website address: www.lernerbooks.co.uk

This edition was updated and edited for UK publication by Discovery Books Ltd.,
Unit 3, 37 Watling Street, Leintwardine, Shropshire SY7 0LW

Words in **bold** type are explained in a glossary on page 31.

British Library Cataloguing in Publication Data

Mitchell, Melanie
   Eating well. - (Pull ahead books. Health)
   1. Food preferences - Juvenile literature 2. Nutrition -
   Juvenile literature
   I. Title
   613.2

   ISBN-13: 978 1 58013 408 8

Printed in China

KNOWSLEY SCHOOL LIBRARY SERVICE	
270520188	
Bertrams	362667
J613.2	

3 8043 27052018 8

Eating Well

by Melanie Mitchell

Series consultants: Sonja Green, MD, and
Distinguished Professor Emerita Ann Nolte, PhD

Lerner Books • London • New York • Minneapolis

There are so many kinds of foods to eat.

How can we choose the right foods
and eat well?

We can pick foods from the six food groups. A food pyramid shows these food groups.

We can pick a variety of foods. Eating food from each of the food groups helps us to stay **healthy**.

We eat bread, cereal, rice and pasta. These are foods in the grains group.

The foods in the grains group give us lots of **energy**. People need energy to work and play each day.

Another food group is the vegetable group. Broccoli and carrots are vegetables. What are some others?

Fruit is another important food group. Apples and bananas are fruit. What fruit can you see here?

Vegetables and fruit give us **vitamins** and **minerals**. Vitamins and minerals help your body grow and stay healthy.

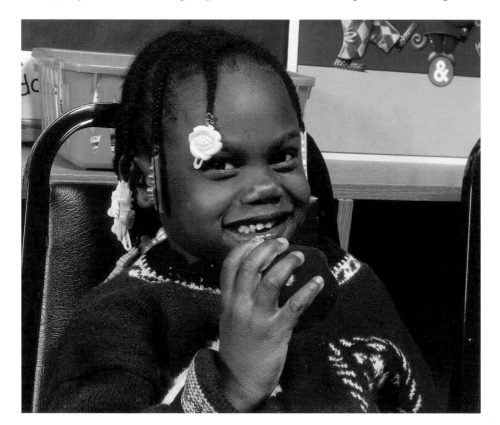

Some fruits, such as oranges, have vitamin C. We need vitamin C to help our skin and bodies heal.

Another food
group is the
dairy group.
It has foods
like milk,
cheese and
yogurt.

Foods made from milk contain calcium. **Calcium** makes bones strong.

The **protein** group has foods like meat, fish, **poultry**, **pulses**, eggs and nuts. These foods contain protein. It helps to keep you strong.

The fats and sugars group has foods like cakes, biscuits, crisps and chocolates. These foods contain a lot of fat and sugar.

We need to drink plenty of water to keep our bodies healthy.

Eating too little or too much of some foods is not healthy. How can we eat the right amount?

Children need 5 portions of grain foods a day.

One slice of bread equals 1 portion from the grains group. So does two heaped spoons of rice or pasta.

You should eat 5 portions of vegetables and fruit each day. Two broccolli florets or three spoons of chopped carrots is one portion.

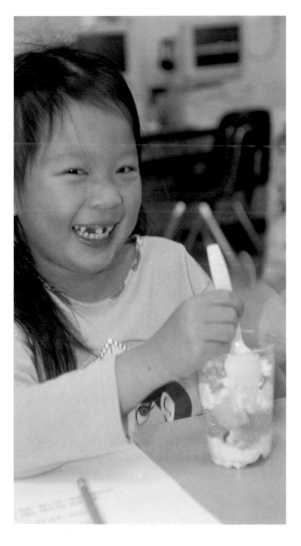

One apple or a handful of grapes is one portion of fruit. People can eat fresh fruit, dried fruit, tinned fruit, or drink fruit juice to stay healthy.

You should
have about 2
to 3 portions
of dairy foods
each day.
This can be
two glasses
of milk or a
bowl of
yogurt.

You need 3 portions from the proteins group each day. Each of these foods equals 1 portion.

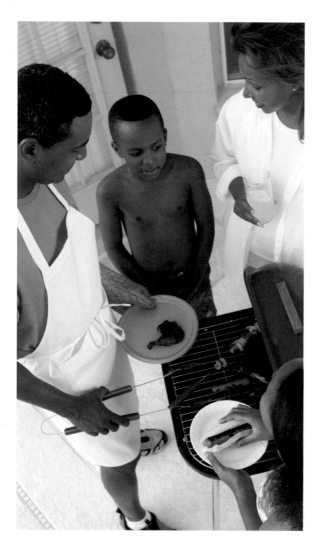

Meat with only a little fat on it is a good choice. Grilling, baking or roasting meat reduces the fat that you eat.

Fats and sugars are in a lot of foods.
You should only eat a little bit of food
from the fats and sugar food group.

Food gives us energy to run and play.
Keeping active helps us use all the
food we eat.

Exercising and eating a variety of foods keeps us healthy.

Did You Know that...?

■ Some vegetables have protein. Peanuts, soya beans and black beans are in the vegetables group. But they also have protein. Foods like peanut butter or tofu or black beans and rice all have protein.

■ Wholegrain foods are good for you. Wholewheat bread, oatmeal and brown rice are kinds of wholegrain foods.

■ Vitamin A helps your eyes work. It can even help you see better at night! Carrots and sweet potatoes have vitamin A.

■ Your body needs iron. Iron is a mineral in food. It helps your body use **oxygen** and gives you energy. Iron is in broccoli, potato skins, raisins, beef and tuna fish.

■ Some meals contain most of the food groups. A sandwich can be made with bread, lettuce, tomatoes, cheese and ham. Can you think of any other meals that have something from nearly all the food groups?

Food Pyramid

Fats and Sugar Group
Only eat foods from this group as a treat.

Protein Group
You should have a protein food as part of every meal.

Dairy Group
Drinking a glass of milk every day will help to make your teeth and bones strong.

Fruit Group
Fruit is packed with vitamins that help your body work.

Vegetables Group
Vegetables contain vitamins and fibre to help keep your body healthy.

Grains Group
Make sure half the grains you eat are wholegrains.

Books and Websites

Books

Llewellyn, Claire. *Your Food* (Look After Yourself) Franklin Watts Ltd, 2004.

Rees, Jonathan. *It's Your Health!: Eating Properly* (It's Your Health) Franklin Watts Ltd, 2004.

Royston, Angela. *Healthy Food* (Look After Yourself) Heinemann, 2003.

Royston, Angela. *What Should We Eat?* (Stay Healthy!) Heinemann, 2006.

Spilsbury, Louise. *Why Should I Eat This Carrot?: And Other Questions About Healthy Eating* (Body Matters) Heinemann, 2003.

Websites

BBC Schools - Importance of food and exercise
http://www.bbc.co.uk/northernireland/schools/4_11/uptoyou/index.shtml

Welltown
http://www.welltown.gov.uk/school/dining.html

Glossary

calcium: a part of some foods that keeps teeth and bones healthy

energy: power within the body that lets it move and be active

healthy: being in good condition physically and mentally or something that helps you stay in good condition

minerals: something found in food that keeps us healthy. Calcium is a mineral.

oxygen: something people take in when they breathe. Living things need oxygen.

poultry: birds raised for their eggs and meat

protein: something in foods that helps keep muscles and other parts of your body healthy and strong

pulses: seeds and beans like lentils, chickpeas and butter beans

vitamins: a part of food that keeps you healthy and helps your body work

Index

Photo Acknowledgements

The photographs in this book appear with the permission of: © Ryan McVay/Getty Images, front cover; © Sam Lund/Independent Picture Service, p. 3; © PhotoDisc/Getty Images, pp. 4, 8, 9, 11, 13, 26; © Royalty-Free/CORBIS, pp. 5, 7, 17; © Comstock/SuperStock, pp. 6, 12, 14; © Todd Strand/Independent Picture Service, pp. 10, 18, 19, 20, 23; © Bobby Humphrey/Discovery Books, pp. 15, 25; © Chris Fairclough/Discovery Picture Library, p. 16; U.S. Department of Agriculture, p. 21; © Stock Image/SuperStock, p. 22; © age foto-stock/SuperStock, p. 24; © Charles Gupton/CORBIS, p. 27. Illustration on p. 29 appears courtesy of Joanna Williams.